MR

Also published by Oxford University Press:

Zbigniew Herbert (translated by John Carpenter and Bogdana Carpenter)
  Selected Poems, 1977
  Report from the Besieged City and Other Poems, 1987

MR COGITO

Zbigniew Herbert

Translated from the Polish by
John Carpenter and Bogdana Carpenter

OXFORD UNIVERSITY PRESS
1993

Oxford University Press, Walton Street, Oxford OX2 6DP

Oxford New York Toronto
Delhi Bombay Calcutta Madras Karachi
Kuala Lumpur Singapore Hong Kong Tokyo
Nairobi Dar es Salaam Cape Town
Melbourne Auckland Madrid
and associated companies in
Berlin Ibadan

Oxford is a trade mark of Oxford University Press

First published in English translation by
Oxford University Press 1993

Published in the United States and Canada by
The Ecco Press, New York

British Library Cataloguing in Publication Data
Data available

Library of Congress Cataloging in Publication Data
Herbert, Zbigniew.
[Pan Cogito. English]
Mr Cogito / Zbigniew Herbert; translated from the Polish by
John and Bogdana Carpenter.
p.   cm.
Translation of: Pan Cogito.
I. Title.
PG7167.E67P3613 1993   891.8'517—dc20   92-34888
ISBN 0-19-282873-8

1 3 5 7 9 10 8 6 4 2

Typeset by J&L Composition Ltd, Filey, North Yorkshire
Printed in Hong Kong

CONTENTS

MR COGITO

MR COGITO LOOKS AT HIS FACE IN THE MIRROR

Who wrote our faces certainly chicken pox
marking its 'o' with a calligraphic pen
but who gave me the double chin
which glutton when all my soul
yearned for asceticism why are the eyes
set so close after all it was he not me
who strained his eyes in the underbrush for the invasion of the
                                                              Venedas
ears protruding too far two shells of skin
probably a legacy from an ancestor who caught the echo
of a rumbling procession of mammoths over the steppe

the forehead not too high very few thoughts
—women gold earth don't let yourself be knocked from the horse
the prince thought for them and wind carried them on the roads
they tore at walls with their fingers and suddenly with a great cry
fell into emptiness in order to return in me

and yet I bought in salons
powders ointments mixtures
rouge for nobility
I applied the marble greenness of Veronese to my eyes
steeped my ears in Mozart
perfected my nostrils with the fragrance of old books

in front of the mirror the inherited face
old meats fermenting in a bag
passions and medieval sins
paleolithic hunger and fear
the apple falls next to the apple tree
the body linked to the chain of species

this is how I lost the tournament with my face

3

ABOUT MR COGITO'S TWO LEGS

The left leg normal
one could say optimistic
a little too short
boyish
with exuberant muscles
and a well-shaped calf

the right leg
God help us—
thin
with two scars
one along the Achilles tendon
the other oval
pale pink
shameful reminder of an escape

the left
inclined to leap
ready to dance
loving life too much
to expose itself

the right
nobly rigid
sneering at danger

in this way
on two legs
the left which can be compared to Sancho Panza
and the right
recalling the wandering knight
Mr Cogito
goes
through the world
staggering slightly

REMEMBERING MY FATHER

His face severe in clouds above the waters of childhood
so rarely did he hold my warm head in his hands
given to belief not forgiving faults
because he cleared out woods and straightened paths
he carried the lantern high when we entered the night

I thought I would sit at his right hand
and we would separate light from darkness
and judge those of us who live
—it happened otherwise

a junk-dealer carried his throne on a hand-cart
and the deed of ownership the map of our kingdom

he was born for a second time slight very fragile
with transparent skin hardly perceptible cartilage
he diminished his body so I might receive it

in an unimportant place there is shadow under a stone

he himself grows in me we eat our defeats
we burst out laughing
when they say how little is needed
to be reconciled

MOTHER

He fell from her knees like a ball of yarn.
He unwound in a hurry and ran blindly away.
She held the beginning of life. She would wind it
on her finger like a ring, she wanted to preserve him.
He was rolling down steep slopes, sometimes
he was climbing up. He would come back tangled, and be silent.
Never will he return to the sweet throne of her knees.

The stretched-out hands are alight in the darkness
like an old town.

SISTER

Thanks to a slight difference in age to childish intimacy
a common bath the mystery of fluffy hair and soft skin
the small Cogito discovered—he could be his sister
(it was as simple as changing places at table
when the parents were out and grandmother permitted everything)
and she the owner of his name his bow his man's bicycle well even
                                                            his nose
luckily they had different noses the lack of physical resemblance
let them avoid dramatic consequences
it ended with touch touch didn't open
and the young Cogito remained in the limits of his own skin

a grain of doubt the undermining of the *principium individuationis*
was deeply implanted however and one afternoon
the thirteen-year-old Cogito saw on the Street of the Legions
a horse cabman
he felt he was him so completely
that a red moustache broke out
and the cold whip burned his hand

MR COGITO AND THE PEARL

Sometimes Mr Cogito recalls, not without emotion, his youthful attempts at perfection, those juvenile *per aspera ad astra*. One day a small pebble happened to fall inside his shoe as he was hurrying to classes. It maliciously worked its way between raw flesh and his sock. Common sense suggested that he get rid of the intruder, but the principle of *amor fati* demanded on the contrary that he endure it. He chose the second, heroic solution.

In the beginning it didn't seem dangerous, a nuisance and nothing more. But after a while the heel appeared in his field of consciousness— it was at the moment when the young Cogito was trying to grasp with great effort what the professor was saying about Plato's concept of ideas. The heel grew, swelled, pulsated, from pale pink it became scarlet red like a setting sun, and pushed out of his head not only Plato's idea but all other ideas as well.

In the evening before going to bed he emptied the foreign body from his sock. It was a small, cold, yellow grain of sand. The heel on the contrary was large, burning, and dark with pain.

SENSE OF IDENTITY

If he had a sense of identity it was probably with a stone
with sandstone not too crumbly light light-grey
which has a thousand eyes of flint
(a senseless comparison the stone sees with its skin)
if he had a feeling of profound union it was exactly with a stone

it wasn't at all the idea of invariability the stone
was changeable lazy in the sunshine brightened like the moon
at the approach of a storm it became dark slate like a cloud
then greedily drank the rain and this wrestling with water
sweet annihilation the struggle of forces clash of elements
the loss of one's own nature drunken stability
were both beautiful and humiliating

so at last it would become sober in the air dried by thunder
embarrassing sweat the passing mist of erotic fervours

MR COGITO THINKS OF RETURNING
TO THE CITY WHERE HE WAS BORN

If I went back there
probably I wouldn't find
even a shadow from my house
nor the trees of childhood
nor the cross with an iron plate
the bench where I whispered incantations
chestnuts and blood
nor a single thing that is ours

all that was saved
is a flagstone
with a circle drawn in chalk
I stand in the centre
on one leg
the moment before jumping

I cannot grow up
although years go by
and planets and wars
roar above

I stand in the centre
motionless as a statue
on a single leg
before the leap to finality

the circle of chalk turns red
like old blood
while all around
piles of ash are growing
up to my shoulders
up to my mouth

MR COGITO MEDITATES ON SUFFERING

All attempts to remove
the so-called cup of bitterness—
by reflection
frenzied actions on behalf of homeless cats
deep breathing
religion—
failed

one must consent
gently bend the head
not wring the hands
make use of the suffering gently moderately
like an artificial limb
without false shame
but also without unnecessary pride

do not brandish the stump
over the heads of others
don't knock with the white cane
against the windows of the well-fed

drink the essence of bitter herbs
but not to the dregs
leave carefully
a few sips for the future

accept
but simultaneously
isolate within yourself
and if it is possible
create from the matter of suffering
a thing or a person

play
with it
of course
play

entertain it
very cautiously
like a sick child
forcing at last
with silly tricks
a faint
smile

THE ABYSS OF MR COGITO

At home it is always safe
but just beyond the door
as soon as Mr Cogito
leaves for a walk in the morning
he encounters—an abyss

it is not the abyss of Pascal
it is not the abyss of Dostoevsky
it is an abyss
to Mr Cogito's measure

its particular features
are not bottomlessness
or the terror it causes

it follows him like a shadow
stops at the bakery
in the park it reads the newspaper
over Mr Cogito's shoulder

as bothersome as eczema
attached to him like a dog
too shallow to engulf
head arms and legs

one day perhaps
the abyss will grow up
the abyss will mature
and become serious

if only he knew
what water it drinks
what grain to feed it

now
Mr Cogito
could gather
a few handfuls of sand
fill it up
but he does not do this

when
he returns home
he leaves the abyss
just outside the door
covering it carefully
with a small piece of old cloth

MR COGITO AND PURE THOUGHT

Mr Cogito tries
to attain pure thought
at least before sleep

but the attempt
carries the seeds of its own defeat

as he arrives
at the state when thought is like water
vast and pure water
at an indifferent shore

the water suddenly ruffles over
and a wave brings
tin cans
driftwood
a tuft of hair

to tell the truth Mr Cogito
is not completely without fault
he was unable to detach
his inner eye
from the mailbox
the smell of the sea was in his nostrils
crickets tickled his ear
and he felt her absent fingers under his ribs

he was ordinary like everyone else
with furnished thoughts
the hand's skin on the back of a chair
a furrow of tenderness
on a cheek

sometime
sometime later
when he grows cold
he will reach the state of satori

and be as the masters recommend
empty and
amazing

MR COGITO READS THE NEWSPAPER

On the first page
a report of the killing of 120 soldiers

the war lasted a long time
you could get used to it

     close alongside
     the news of a sensational crime
     with a portrait of the murderer

     the eye of Mr Cogito
     slips indifferently
     over the soldiers' hecatomb
     to plunge with delight
     into the description of everyday horror

     a thirty-year-old farm labourer
     under the stress of nervous depression
     killed his wife
     and two small children

     it is described with precision
     the course of the murder
     the position of the bodies
     and other details

     for 120 dead
     you search on a map in vain

     too great a distance
     covers them like a jungle

     they don't speak to the imagination
     there are too many of them
     the numeral zero at the end
     changes them into an abstraction

     a subject for meditation:
     the arithmetic of compassion

MR COGITO AND THE MOVEMENT
OF THOUGHTS

Thoughts cross the mind
says the popular expression

the popular expression
overestimates the movement of thoughts

most of them
stand motionless
in the middle of a dull landscape
of ashy hills
parched trees

sometimes they come
to the bursting river of another's thoughts
they stand on the shore
on one leg
like hungry herons

with sadness
they remember the dried-up springs

they turn in a circle
searching for grain

they don't cross
because they will never arrive
they don't cross
because there is nowhere to go

they sit on stones
wring their hands

under the cloudy
low
sky
of the skull

HOUSES OF THE OUTSKIRTS

On a sunless autumn afternoon Mr Cogito likes
to visit the dirty outskirts of the city. There
is no purer source of melancholy, he says.

Houses of the outskirts with black-ringed windows
houses coughing quietly
shivers of plaster
houses with thin hair
sick complexion

only the chimneys dream
the lean complaint
reaches the edge of the forest
a shore of vast water

    I would like to invent names for you
    to fill you with the scent of India
    the fire of the Bosporus
    murmur of waterfalls

houses of the outskirts with sunken temples
houses chewing breadcrusts
cold as the sleep of a paralytic
whose stairways are palmtrees of dust
houses always for sale
inns of misfortune
houses which were never at the theatre

    the rats of the houses of the outskirts
    lead them to the shore of the ocean
    let them sit in the hot sand
    let them watch the tropical night
    let the wave reward them with a stormy ovation
    as befits only wasted lives

MR COGITO'S ALIENATIONS

Mr Cogito holds in his arms
the warm amphora of a head

the rest of the body is hidden
only touch sees it

he looks at the sleeping head
strange yet full of tenderness

once again
he notices with amazement
that someone exists outside of him
impenetrable
like a stone

with limits
which open
only for a moment
then the sea casts it up
on the rocky shore

with its own blood
strange sleep
armed with its own skin

Mr Cogito removes
the sleeping head
gently

not to leave
on the cheek
the imprints of fingers

and he goes away
alone
into the lime of the sheets

MR COGITO LOOKS AT A DECEASED FRIEND

He breathed heavily

the crisis was supposed to be at night
it was twelve noon
Mr Cogito walked into the corridor
to smoke a cigarette

first he straightened the pillow
and smiled at his friend

he breathed heavily

his fingers
were moving
on the sheet

when he returned
his friend was no longer there
something else lay
in his place
with a twisted head
and goggle eyes

normal comings and goings
the doctor hurried in
pushed in a syringe
which filled
with dark blood

Mr Cogito
waited a moment longer
staring at what was left

it was empty
as a sack
shrinking
more and more
squeezed by invisible tongs
crushed by a different time

if only he turned to stone
into a heavy sculpture of marble
indifferent and noble
what a relief would it be

he lay on a narrow promontory
of destruction
torn off from the trunk
abandoned like a cocoon

dinner
the plates tolled
an Angelus
the angels did not descend

the Upanishads comforted

when his speech
enters thought
thought enters breath
breath enters fire
and fire the highest deity
then he is no longer
able to comprehend

so he did not comprehend
and he was impenetrable
with a bundle of coarse mystery
at the gates of the valley

ORDINARINESS OF THE SOUL

In the morning mice scamper
over the head
over the floor of the head
shreds of conversations
scraps of a poem
the room's muse
enters
in a blue apron
she sweeps

such important guests
visit my master
Heraclitus the Ephesian for example
or the prophet Isaiah

today no one rings

the master paces about impatiently
talks to himself
tears up innocent papers

in the evening goes out in an unknown direction

the muse unties her blue apron
rests her elbows on the window sill
leans out
waits
for her sergeant
with red moustaches

LATE AUTUMNAL POEM OF MR COGITO
DESTINED FOR WOMEN'S MAGAZINES

The time of apples falling leaves still put up a defence
in the morning heavier and heavier fog the air grows bald
last grains of honey first reds of the maples
a fox killed on a field space reverberating with shots

apples will go underground trunks come up to the eyes
leaves will be stored in chests and the wood speak
now we can distinctly hear the planets as they move
a high moon rises accept the glaze over your eyes

TO TAKE OBJECTS OUT

To take objects out of their royal silence one must use either a stratagem or a crime. The frozen lake of a door is broken by the knocking of a carouser, a goblet dropped on the parquet floor gives an abrupt shriek like a glass bird, and a house which has been set on fire talks with the loquacious language of flames, with the language of a breathless epic poet, about what the bed, the chests, and the curtain were silent.

MR COGITO CONSIDERS THE DIFFERENCE BETWEEN THE HUMAN VOICE AND THE VOICE OF NATURE

The oration of the worlds is untiring

I can repeat all of it from the beginning
with a pen inherited from a goose and Homer
with a diminished spear
stand in front of the elements

I can repeat all of it from the beginning
the hand will lose to the mountain
the throat is weaker than a spring
I will not outshout the sand
not with saliva tie a metaphor
the eye with a star
and with the ear next to a stone
I won't bring out stillness
from the grainy silence

and yet I gathered so many words in one line—longer than all the
lines of my palm and therefore longer than fate in a line aiming
beyond in a line blossoming in a luminous line in a line which is to
save me in the column of my life—straight as courage a line strong
as love—but it was hardly a miniature of the horizon

and the thunderbolts of flowers continue to roll on the oration of
                                        grass the oration of clouds
choruses of trees mutter rock blazes quietly
the ocean extinguishes the sunset the day swallows the night and on
                                        the pass of the winds
new light rises

                and morning mist lifts the shield of islands

SEQUOIA

Gothic towers of needles in the valley of a stream
not far from Mount Tamalpais where in the morning and
evening thick fog comes like the wrath and passion of the ocean

in this reservation of giants they display a cross-section of a tree
                                the coppery stump of the West
with immense regular veins like rings on water
and someone perverse has inscribed the dates of human history
an inch from the middle of the stump the fire of distant Rome
                                    under Nero
in the middle the battle of Hastings the night expedition of the
                                    drakkars
panic of the Anglo-Saxons the death of the unfortunate Harold
it is told with a compass
and finally right next to the beach of the bark the landing of the
                                  Allies in Normandy

the Tacitus of this tree was a geometrician and he did not know
                                  adjectives
he did not know syntax expressing terror he did not know any words
therefore he counted added years and centuries as if to say there is
                                  nothing
beyond birth and death nothing only birth and death
and inside the bloody pulp of the sequoia

THOSE WHO LOST

Those who lost dance with bells at their legs
in fetters of comic costumes in the feathers of a croaked eagle
dust of compassion flies over the small square
as a cinematic carbine shoots gently and accurately

they lift an axe of tin with a bow light as an eyebrow they murder
leaves and shadows
and only the drum booms recalling ancient pride and wrath

they abandoned history and entered the laziness of a display-case
they lie in a glass tomb next to faithful stones

those who lost—they are vendors next to the Governor's Palace in
Santa Fe
(a long one-storey building of warm scorched dark ochre
columns of wood jutting beams of a ceiling where a sharp shadow
hangs)
they sell beads amulets of the god of rain and fire a miniature of the
temple of Kiva
with two straws of a ladder pointing up where the harvest descends

buy the god echo it is cheap and expressively silent
as it hesitates on a hand stretched out to us
from the stone age

27

MR COGITO LAMENTS THE PETTINESS OF DREAMS

Even dreams become smaller
     where are our grandmothers' and grandfathers'
        entranced processions
when colourful as birds light-hearted as birds they mounted high
on an imperial staircase a thousand chandeliers were glowing
and grandfather familiar now only with the cane pressing his side
a silver sword and unloved grandmother who was so kind
she put on for him the face of their first love

     to them
Isaiah spoke from clouds that looked like clouds of tobacco smoke
      and they saw how Saint Teresa
white as a wafer carried a real basket with dry twigs

their terror was as great as the Tartar Horde
and their happiness in dream was like golden rain

my dream—a doorbell I am shaving in the bathroom I open the door
the collector hands me a bill for gas and electricity
I have no money return to the bathroom meditating
on the number 63.50
       I raise my eyes and see in the mirror
my face that is so real I wake with a shout

if I dreamt at least once of the executioner's red jacket
or the necklace of a queen I would be grateful to dreams

MR COGITO AND A POET OF A CERTAIN AGE

1

A poet after the prime of life
a peculiar phenomenon

2

he looks at himself in the mirror
he breaks the mirror

3

on a moonless night
he drowns his birth certificate in a black pond

4

he watches the young
imitates the way they swing their hips

5

he chairs a meeting
of independent Trotskyites
incites them to acts of arson

6

he writes letters
to the President of the Solar System
full of intimate confessions

7

the poet of a certain age
in the middle of an uncertain age

8

instead of cultivating
pansies and onomatopoeias
he plants prickly exclamations
invectives and treatises

9

he reads one after the other
Isaiah and *Das Kapital*
then in the fervour of discussion
confuses his quotations

10

a poet at an unclear time of life
between departing Eros
and Thanatos who has not yet risen from his stone

11

he smokes hashish
but does not see
infinity
or flowers
or waterfalls
he sees a procession
of hooded monks
climbing a rocky mountain
with extinguished torches

12

the poet of a certain age
remembers his warm childhood
his exuberant youth
inglorious manhood

13

he plays
the game of Freud
he plays
the game of hope
he plays
at the red and black
he plays
at flesh and bones
he plays and loses
he bursts out with insincere laughter

14

only now does he understand his father
he cannot forgive his sister
who ran away with an actor
he envies his younger brother
bent over the photograph of his mother
he tries once more
to persuade her to conceive

15

his dreams
pubertal not serious
the priest from catechism
protruding objects
and the unattainable Jadzia

16

at dawn he looks
at his hand
he is surprised by his own skin
similar to bark

17

against the young blue sky
the white tree of his veins

MR COGITO AND POP

During a pop concert
Mr Cogito reflects
on the aesthetics of noise

an idea in itself quite
attractive

to be a god
means to hurl thunderbolts

or less theologically
to swallow the tongue of the elements

to replace Homer
with an earthquake
Horace
with a stone avalanche

to drag from the entrails
what is in the entrails
fright and hunger

to strip the path
of the gut
to strip the path
of breathing
to bare the path
of desire

to play on the red throat
frantic love songs

2

the difficulty is
that the shriek eludes form
is poorer than the voice
which ascends
and falls

the shriek touches silence
but through hoarseness
not through the will
to describe silence

it is garishly dark
from powerlessness of articulation

has rejected the grace of humour
as it does not know half-tones

is like a blade
driven into mystery
but doesn't entwine
around the mystery
doesn't come to know its shapes

it expresses the truth of feelings
from wilderness parks

searches for a lost paradise
in new jungles of order

prays for a violent death
and this will be granted

MR COGITO ON MAGIC

I

Mircea Eliade is right
we are—despite everything
an advanced society

magic and gnosis
flourish as never before

artificial paradises
artificial hells
are being sold on the street corner

plastic instruments of torture
have been discovered in Amsterdam

a maid from Massachusetts
received a baptism of blood

seventh day catatonics
stand on the runways
the fourth dimension will snatch them away
an ambulance with a hoarse siren

along Telegraph Avenue
shoals of beards swim
in the sweet smell of nirvana

Joe Dove dreamt
he was god
and god was nothingness

he floated down slowly like a feather
from the Eiffel Tower

a teenage philosopher
disciple of de Sade
expertly cuts
the belly of a pregnant woman
and with blood paints on a wall
prophecies of extermination

there are also oriental orgies
forced and somewhat boring

2

fortunes grow out of this
branches of industry
branches of crime

industrious ships sail
to bring new spices

engineers of visual debauchery
toil without rest

breathless alchemists of hallucination
produce
new thrills
new colours
new moans

and an art is born
of aggressive epilepsy

in time
the depravers will turn grey
and think of atonement

then new prisons
will arise
new asylums
new cemeteries

but this is still a vision
of a better future

for the time being
magic
flourishes
as never before

MR COGITO ENCOUNTERS A STATUETTE
OF THE GREAT MOTHER IN THE LOUVRE

This small cosmology of burnt clay
a little larger than the hand comes from Boeotia
on top a head like the holy mountain of Meru
from which hair flows—great rivers of the earth
the neck is the sky pulsating with warmth
sleepless constellations
a necklace of clouds

> send us holy water of harvests
> you with leaves growing from your fingers
> we who are born of clay
> like the ibis snake and grass
> we want you to hold us
> in your strong palms

on her belly the square earth
guarded by a double sun

> we don't want other gods our fragile house of air
> a stone a tree simple names of things are enough
> carry us carefully from night to night
> then blow out our senses at the threshold of the question

in a glass case the deserted Mother
is looking with the surprised eye of a star

HISTORY OF THE MINOTAUR

The true history of the prince Minotaur is told in the script Linear A, which has not yet been deciphered. Notwithstanding later gossip he was the authentic son of King Minos and Pasiphaë. The boy was born healthy, but with an abnormally large head which the fortune-tellers interpreted as a sign of future wisdom. In reality, with the years the Minotaur grew into a strong and somewhat melancholy—nitwit. The king decided to turn him over to the priesthood. But the priests explained that they could not admit the abnormal prince because it would lower the authority of religion, which had already been damaged by the invention of the wheel.

Consequently, Minos brought over an engineer then fashionable in Greece, Daedalus—creator of a noted branch of pedagogical architecture. This is how the labyrinth was built. By a system of corridors, from the simplest to the more complicated, by a difference in levels and a staircase of abstractions it was supposed to initiate the prince Minotaur into the principles of correct thinking.

So the miserable prince mooned about in the corridors of induction and deduction, pushed by his preceptors; he looked at the instructive frescoes with a vacant stare. He didn't understand a thing.

When King Minos had exhausted all his resources he decided to get rid of the disgrace to the family. He brought over (also from Greece, which was famous for capable people) the skilful murderer Theseus. And Theseus killed the Minotaur. On this point, myth and history are in agreement.

Through the labyrinth—by now an unnecessary school primer—Theseus returns carrying the huge, blood-stained head of the Minotaur, its eyes bulging, where for the first time wisdom began to sprout—which usually is brought by experience.

OLD PROMETHEUS

He writes his memoirs. He is trying to explain the place of the hero in a system of necessities, to reconcile the notions of existence and fate that contradict each other.

Fire is crackling gaily in the fireplace, in the kitchen his wife bustles about—an exalted girl who did not bear him a son, but is convinced she will pass into history anyway. Preparations for supper: the local parson is coming, and the pharmacist, now the closest friend of Prometheus.

The fire blazes up. On the wall, a stuffed eagle and a letter of gratitude from the tyrant of the Caucasus, who successfully burned down a town in revolt because of Prometheus' discovery.

Prometheus laughs quietly. Now it is the only way of expressing his disagreement with the world.

CALIGULA

Reading old chronicles poems and lives Mr Cogito
sometimes experiences the physical presence of persons
long dead

CALIGULA SPEAKS:

of all the citizens of Rome
I loved only one
Incitatus—the horse

when he entered the senate
the spotless toga of his coat
glistened immaculately among the purple-trimmed cowardly
                                                    murderers

Incitatus was full of qualities
he never gave speeches
a stoic nature
I think he read the philosophers in his stable at night

I loved him so much one day I decided to crucify him
but his noble anatomy resisted it

he accepted the rank of consul indifferently
he performed his duties excellently
that is he didn't perform them at all

it was impossible to incite him to a lasting bond of love
with my second wife Caesonia
thus unfortunately a line of Caesar-Centaurs did not come
                                                    into being

this is why Rome fell

I decided to appoint him a god
but on the ninth day before the calends of February
Cherea Cornelius Sabinus and other fools hindered these
                                                    pious intentions

calmly he accepted the news of my death

he was thrown out of the palace and condemned to exile

he bore this blow with dignity

he died without progeny
slaughtered by a thick-skinned butcher from the locality of Ancium

about the posthumous fate of his meat
Tacitus is silent

HAKELDAMA

The priests have a problem
on the borderline of ethics and accounting

what to do with the silver coins
Judas threw at their feet

the sum was registered
under the heading of expenses
chroniclers will write it down
under the heading of legend

to record it under the rubric
unexpected earnings would be wrong
to put it in the treasury dangerous
it might infect the silver

it wouldn't be right
to buy a candle-holder with it for the temple
or give it to the poor

after long consultation
they decide to buy a potter's field
and build a cemetery
for pilgrims

to give—so to speak
money for death
back to death

the solution
was tactful
therefore why
does the name of this place
rend the air for centuries
Hakeldama
Hakeldama
field of blood

MR COGITO TELLS ABOUT THE
TEMPTATION OF SPINOZA

Baruch Spinoza of Amsterdam
was seized by a desire to reach God

in the attic
cutting lenses
he suddenly pierced a curtain
and stood face to face

he spoke for a long time
(and as he so spoke
his mind enlarged
and his soul)
he posed questions
about the nature of man

—distracted God stroked his beard

—he asked about the first cause

—God looked into infinity

—he asked about the final cause

—God cracked his knuckles
cleared his throat

when Spinoza became silent
God spake

—you talk nicely Baruch
I like your geometric Latin
and the clear syntax
the symmetry of your arguments

let's speak however
about Things Truly
Great

—look at your hands
cut and trembling

—you destroy your eyes
in the darkness

—you are badly nourished
you dress shabbily

—buy a new house
forgive the Venetian mirrors
that they repeat surfaces

—forgive flowers in the hair
the drunken song

—look after your income
like your colleague Descartes

—be cunning
like Erasmus

—dedicate a treatise
to Louis XIV
he won't read it anyway

—calm
the rational fury
thrones will fall because of it
and stars turn black

—think
about the woman
who will give you a child

—you see Baruch
we are speaking about Great Things

—I want to be loved
by the uneducated and the violent
they are the only ones
who really hunger for me

now the curtain falls
Spinoza remains alone

he does not see the golden cloud
the light on the heights

he see darkness

he hears the creaking of the stairs
footsteps going down

GEORG HEYM—THE ALMOST
METAPHYSICAL ADVENTURE

I

If it is true
an image precedes thought
one would believe
that the ideas of Heym
originated while ice skating

—the ease of moving
over the icy surface

he was there and here
he circled around the moving centre
he wasn't a planet
nor a bell
nor a farmer tied to his plough

—the relativity of movement
mirror-like interpenetration of systems

the closer left-hand shore
(the red roofs of Gatow)
was flying backwards
like a violently tugged tablecloth
while the right-hand shore
stayed (apparently) in place

—the overthrow of determinism
marvellous coexistence of possibilities

—my greatness—
Heym was saying to himself
(he was now gliding backwards
with the left leg raised)
is based on the discovery
that in the contemporary world
there are no direct results
no tyranny of sequence
dictatorship of causality
all thoughts

actions
objects
phenomena
lie side by side
like the traces of skates
on a white surface

a weighty assertion
for theoretical physics
a dangerous assertion
for the theory of poetry

2

those who stood on the right shore
didn't notice the disappearance of Heym

the high school student passing him
saw everything in reverse order:

white sweater
trousers fastened below the knee
with two bone buttons

calves in orange stockings
the skates the cause of the accident

two policeman pushed a path
through the crowd of onlookers
standing over the hole in the ice

(it looked like the entrance to a dungeon
like the cold mouth of a mask)

licking their pencils
they tried to record the event
to introduce order
according to the obsolete
logic of Aristotle

with the slow-minded
indifference of authority
for the discoverer
and his thoughts
which were now
wandering helplessly
under the ice

SOMETIMES MR COGITO RECEIVES
STRANGE LETTERS

Mrs Amelia from Darmstadt
asks for help
in finding her great-great-grandfather
Ludwig I

he was lost
like so many others
in the tumult of the war

he was seen
for the last time
on a family estate
in the region of Jelenia Góra

Mr Cogito
remembers well
the severe winter of 1944
full of fires

the great-great-grandfather
Grossherzog by profession
lived at the time
inside a frame

he stood
before a garden house
in a uniform
white trousers

on the right
a broken column
in the background
a dark stormy sky
with a bright stripe on the horizon

Mr Cogito
thinks
without a trace of irony
about the death of the great-great-grandfather

didn't he lose
his cold blood
when the conflagration
was sitting astride the parapet

didn't he cry out
as he was dragged across the courtyard

didn't he fall
pleading on his knees
when they aimed
at the great star on his chest

the imagination
of Mr Cogito
is small
like a stretcher-bearer
lost in fog

he does not see
the face
the uniform
white trousers

he sees only
the dark stormy sky
with a bright stripe on the horizon

MEDITATIONS OF MR COGITO ON
REDEMPTION

He should not have sent his son

too many have seen
his son's pierced hands
his ordinary skin

      it was written
      to reconcile us
      by the worst reconciliation

too many nostrils
have breathed with delight
the odour of his fear

      one should not descend
      low
      fraternize with blood

he should not have sent his son
it was better to reign
in a baroque palace made out of marble clouds
on a throne of terror
with a sceptre of death

MR COGITO SEEKS ADVICE

So many books dictionaries
obese encyclopedias
but no one to give advice

they explored the sun
the moon the stars
they lost me

my soul
refuses the consolation
of knowledge

      so it wanders at night
      on the roads of the fathers

      and look
      the small town of Braclaw
      among black sunflowers

      this place which we abandoned
      this place which shouts

      it is the sabbath
      as always on the sabbath
      a new Sky appears

      —I'm looking for you rabbi

      —he isn't here—
      say the Hasidim
      —he is in the world of Sheol

      —he had a beautiful death
      say the Hasidim
      —very beautiful
      as if he passed
      from one corner
      to another corner
      all black
      he had in his hand
      a flaming Torah

—I'm looking for you rabbi

—behind which firmament
did you hide your wise ear

—my heart hurts rabbi
—I have troubles

perhaps rabbi Nachman
could give me advice
but how can I find him
among so many ashes

MR COGITO'S GAME

I

The favourite amusement
of Mr Cogito
is the game Kropotkin

it has many merits
the game Kropotkin

it liberates the historical imagination
the feeling of solidarity
it is played in the fresh air
it abounds in dramatic episodes
its rules are noble
despotism always loses

on the big board of the imagination
Mr Cogito sets the pieces

the king designates
Peter Kropotkin in the Pietropavlovsk Fortress
the bishops are three soldiers and a sentry
the castle is the carriage of escape

Mr Cogito can choose
among many roles

he can play
beautiful Sophia Nikolaevna
she smuggles the plan of escape
in a watch case

he can also be the violinist
in the grey cottage
especially rented
opposite the prison
who plays the Abduction from the Seraglio
which means the street is clear

most of all however
Mr Cogito likes
the role of Doctor Orestes Weimar

at the dramatic moment
he distracts the soldier
at the gate by talking

—ever see a microbe Vanya
—never seen one
—and the beast is crawling on your skin
—don't say that your honour
—yes it creeps and has a tail
—big?
—three or four versts

then the fur cap
falls on the sheepish eyes

and already
the game Kropotkin
is moving rapidly along

the king-prisoner runs with great bounds
he struggles for a moment with his flannel bathrobe
the violinist in the grey cottage
plays the Abduction from the Seraglio
voices are heard catch him
Doctor Orestes spins on about microbes

beating of the heart
hobnailed boots on the pavement
at last the carriage of escape
the bishops can't move

Mr Cogito
is happy as a child
again he has won the game Kropotkin

2

so many years
for so many years
Mr Cogito plays

but never
was he attracted by the role
of the hero of the escape

not because of dislike
for the blue blood
of the prince of anarchists
nor abhorrence for his theory
of reciprocal aid

nor is it due to cowardice
Sophia Nikolaevna
the violinist in the grey cottage
Doctor Orestes
also risked their heads

with them however
Mr Cogito
identifies himself almost completely

if it was necessary
he would even be the horse
for the carriage of the fugitive

Mr Cogito
would like to be the intermediary of freedom

to hold the rope of escape
to smuggle the secret message
to give the sign

to trust the heart
the pure impulse of sympathy

but he doesn't want to be responsible for what
will be written in the monthly *Freedom*
by bearded men
of faint imagination

he accepts an inferior role
he won't inhabit history

WHAT MR COGITO THINKS ABOUT HELL

The lowest circle of hell. Contrary to prevailing opinion it is inhabited neither by despots nor matricides, nor even by those who go after the bodies of others. It is the refuge of artists, full of mirrors, musical instruments, and pictures. At first glance this is the most luxurious infernal department, without tar, fire, or physical tortures.

Throughout the year competitions, festivals, and concerts are held here. There is no climax in the season. The climax is permanent and almost absolute. Every few months new trends come into being and nothing, it appears, is capable of stopping the triumphant march of the avant-garde.

Beelzebub loves art. He boasts that already his choruses, his poets, and his painters are nearly superior to those of heaven. He who has better art has better government—that's clear. Soon they will be able to measure their strength against one another at the Festival of the Two Worlds. And then we will see what remains of Dante, Fra Angelico, and Bach.

Beelzebub supports the arts. He provides his artists with calm, good board, and absolute isolation from hellish life.

MR COGITO ON UPRIGHT ATTITUDES

I

In Utica
the citizens
don't want to defend themselves

in town an epidemic broke out
of the instinct of self-preservation

the temple of freedom
has been changed into a flea market

the senate is deliberating
how not to be a senate

the citizens
don't want to defend themselves
they are attending accelerated courses
on falling to the knees

passively they wait for the enemy
they write obsequious speeches
bury their gold

they sew new flags
innocently white
teach their children to lie

they have opened the gates
through which enters now
a column of sand

aside from that as usual
commerce and copulation

2
Mr Cogito
would like to stand
up to the situation

which means
to look fate
straight in the eyes

like Cato the Younger
see in the *Lives*

however he doesn't have
a sword
nor the opportunity
to send his family overseas

therefore he waits like the others
walks back and forth in a sleepless room

despite the advice of the Stoics
he would like to have a body of diamond
and wings

he looks through the window
as the sun of the Republic
is about to set

little remained for him
in fact only
the choice of position
in which he wants to die

the choice of a gesture
choice of a last word

this is why he doesn't go
to bed
in order to avoid
suffocation in sleep

to the end he would like
to stand up to the situation

fate looks him in the eyes
in the place where there was
his head

THE ENVOY OF MR COGITO

Go where those others went to the dark boundary
for the golden fleece of nothingness your last prize

go upright among those who are on their knees
among those with their backs turned and those toppled in the dust

you were saved not in order to live
you have little time you must give testimony

be courageous when the mind deceives you be courageous
in the final account only this is important

and let your helpless Anger be like the sea
whenever you hear the voice of the insulted and beaten

let your sister Scorn not leave you
for the informers executioners cowards—they will win
they will go to your funeral and with relief will throw a lump of earth
the woodborer will write your smoothed-over biography

and do not forgive truly it is not in your power
to forgive in the name of those betrayed at dawn

beware however of unnecessary pride
keep looking at your clown's face in the mirror
repeat: I was called—weren't there better ones than I

beware of dryness of heart love the morning spring
the bird with an unknown name the winter oak

light on a wall the splendour of the sky
they don't need your warm breath
they are there to say: no one will console you

be vigilant—when the light on the mountains gives the sign—arise
                                                        and go
as long as blood turns in the breast your dark star

repeat old incantations of humanity fables and legends
because this is how you will attain the good you will not attain
repeat great words repeat them stubbornly
like those crossing the desert who perished in the sand

and they will reward you with what they have at hand
with the whip of laughter with murder on a garbage heap

go because only in this way will you be admitted to the company of
cold skulls
to the company of your ancestors: Gilgamesh Hector Roland
the defenders of the kingdom without limit and the city of ashes

Be faithful Go